Pokémon ADVENTURES

Volume 14
VIZ Kids Edition

Story by HIDENORI KUSAKA
Art by SATOSHI YAMAMOTO

© 2011 Pokémon.
© 1995–2011 Nintendo/Creatures Inc./GAME FREAK inc.
TM and ® and character names are trademarks of Nintendo.
© 1997 Hidenori KUSAKA and Satoshi YAMAMOTO/Shogakukan
All rights reserved.
Original Japanese edition "POCKET MONSTER SPECIAL"
published by SHOGAKUKAN Inc.

English Adaptation/Gerard Jones
Translation/HC Language Solutions
Touch-up & Lettering/Annaliese Christman
Design/Sam Elzway
Editor/Annette Roman

Printed in the U.S.A.

Published by VIZ Media, LLC
P.O. Box 77010
San Francisco, CA 94107

10 9 8 7 6 5 4 3
First printing, August 2011
Third printing, February 2013

www.vizkids.com
www.viz.com

RATED
A
FOR
ALL AGES

PARENTAL ADVISORY
POKÉMON ADVENTURES
is rated A and is suitable
for readers of all ages.
ratings.viz.com

CHARACTERS THUS FAR

▶ Silver
A Trainer captured and held prisoner by the Masked Man years ago. Since his escape, he has sworn vengeance!

▶ Crystal
A capture specialist who sneaks into the Pokémon League Tournament with Gold...

▶ Gold
A hero leading the battle against the Masked Man to foil his plan of seizing control of time!!

▲ Yellow

▼ Green

◀ Blue

▲ Red

The Gym Leaders

Masked Man
The mysterious ringleader of Neo Team Rocket and undeserving master of Lugia and Ho-Oh!

MAIN
THE JOURNE

Ho-Oh

Lugia

Neo Team Rocket

The Pokémon League Tournam
is reaching a pinnacle of thrills
with spirited battles between
Gym Leaders! Suddenly, an atta
by the Masked Man and Neo Te
Rocket—along with legendary
Pokémon Lugia and Ho-Oh—
creates chaos! Now Gold awaits
his opportunity to strike back ar
capture the Masked Man...

CONTENTS

LUGIA

HO-OH

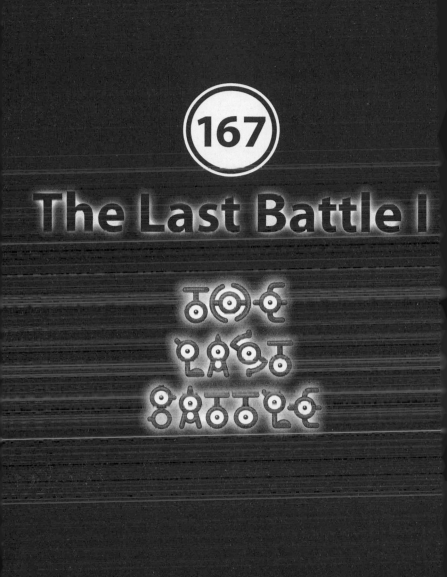

...REATE THIS PECIAL POKÉ BALL?!

CRR

YOU CAPTURED LUGIA AND HO-OH BECAUSE YOU WANTED TO...

...IS WHY... ...YOU CAPTURED THESE POKÉMON?!

SO THIS...

THE POKÉMON LEAGUE... KURT... SILVER—AND THE OTHERS YOU TRAINED... AND EVEN NEO TEAM ROCKET?! ARE THEY ALL JUST MEANS TO AN END?!

WELL ?!

...

WHAT'S WRONG WITH YOU?! ARE POKÉMON JUST **TOOLS** TO YOU?! **MATERIAL** TO MAKE SOMETHING OUT OF?!

17

CONTROLLED BY SOMEONE... WHO IS IN OUR MIDST!!

(158) The Last Battle II

TELL ME...

WSH

BUT CAN YOU PROVE MY THEORY IS WRONG?

I DON'T HAVE ANY PROOF.

WHAT DO YOU MEAN... IN OUR MIDST?! WHAT MAKES YOU SAY THAT?!

NO! IT CAN'T BE!!

170 The Last Battle IV

The Last Battle IV

I CANNOT FORGIVE HIM FOR TREATIN MY BELOVED SUICUNE LIKE THIS...

O
O
B
M

NOW, ELECTRODE... BRING SUICUNE AND THIS YOUNG LADY OUTSIDE THE CRYSTAL WALL.

GOMP

I REMEMBER NOW! THERE'S ONLY ONE PERSON...

I'VE GOT IT...! THAT SOUND I JUST HEARD IS A *CLEAR BELL*!!

AN ITEM THAT CAN NEUTRALIZE THE CRYSTAL WALL FORCE FIELD!

...WHO CAN PASS THROUGH THE CRYSTAL WALL AS HE PLEASES...

...ONE TRAINER WITH A CLEAR BELL...

YES! AN IMPOSSIBLY STRONG FOE!

THAT IMAGE WE SAW ON THE SCREEN JUST NOW... THAT'S THE GUY WHO TRASHED THIS PLACE, RIGHT?!

WE REVERSED THE MAGNET TRAIN AND CAME BACK HERE—AFTER WE DEFEATED THE NEO TEAM ROCKET SOLDIERS!!

DIREC-TOR...

AH, IT'S YOU!

...NOT EVEN HUMAN.

HE'S...

HE KEPT MOVING AND TALKING EVEN AFTER HIS BODY WAS CUT IN HALF AND A HOLE BORED THROUGH HIS STOMACH!

OW!!

YOU SAID... HE STILL MOVED AFTER A HOLE WAS BORED THROUGH HIS STOMACH?!

UH... YES...

UM... THAT HE'S AN IMPOSSIBLY STRONG FOE...?

AFTER THAT!!

DIREC-TOR, WHAT DID YOU JUST SAY?!

WILL AND KAREN ARE ALREADY WAITING FOR ME. GO TO THEM!!

LUGIA!! HO-OH!!

DON'T LET ANYONE GET NEAR ME DURING THAT TIME!

...ALL I NEED TO DO IS PLACE THIS NET INSIDE THE POKÉ BALL TO COMPLETE IT! HAHAHA!

NOW...

HFF... HFF... YOU... MADE IT? NOT SO FAST...

I MADE IT...!!

FWP

THE "SHRINE" REACTS TO THE PHASES OF THE MOON...AND TONIGHT IS THE NIGHT WHEN THE SHRINE WILL SHINE AGAIN.

OU'RE NOT THERE YET!

FWP

FWP

OU ?!

172 The Last Battle VI

AIBO!!

FP

W

AP

FSHOOO

FLOP

KRIIIK

SSSHH

HA HA HA!

THE ARM HE LOST.. GREW BACK?!

I CAN ENDLESSLY REPAIR MY BODY... OR ENLARGE IT!

I GATHER THE WATER IN THE ATMOSPHERE AND FREEZE IT...

...MADE OF ICE?!

A BOD...

72

HAHAHA! SURPRISED AT SUDOBO'S **SPEED**?

IMPOSSIBLE!!

YOU MEAN ...?!

WHEN DID IT GET BEHIND ME?!

AIBO PASSED THE SPEED BOOST FROM **AGILITY** ON TO SUDOBO!!

THAT'S RIGHT!! **BATON PASS**!! A MOVE THAT PASSES ON THE EFFECTS OF A DIFFERENT MOVE!!

YOU USED **PERISH SONG**!!

!!

DELI-BIRD !!

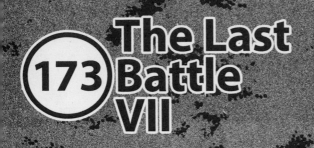

(173) The Last Battle VII

THIS IS...
THE ILEX
FOREST.

ILE

WE NEED TO GET TO THE CENTER OF THIS FOREST. THE...

I'VE GOT TO HURRY!

VMM

SH

82

83

... BIRD !!

B...

YEEE ...!!

HAHA HAHA!! YOU'RE NOT GOING ANY- WHERE!

PSY- CHIC !!

AAAA !!

SHZZ

...TO RECAPTURE LUGIA AND HO-OH TO GATHER THOSE FEATHERS! HAHAHAHA HAHAHAHA !!

AFTER ALL, IT TOOK HIM YEARS ...

HE'LL NEVER FOR- GIVE YOU FOR THAT!

HE WAS VER ANGRY WHEN YO STOLE THOSE FROM HIM, YOU KNOW!!

HAHAHAHAHAHA! SHE SAW THE REAL HO-OH...AND MY XATU USED ITS MYSTIC POWERS TO SHOW HER THE PAST!

HA! SHE FAINTED!

...ENDED UP BEING A GREATER FOE THAN ANY POKÉMON!

THE PHOBIA THAT BEGAN AFTER HO-OH KIDNAPPED HER...

...THINGS MIGHT HAVE BEEN BETTER FOR YOU... BECAUSE YOU WOULDN'T HAVE REMEMBERED ANYTHING! HAHAHAHAHA!

IF YOU'D BEEN AS YOUNG AS LITTLE SILVER WHEN YOU WERE KIDNAPPED...

AT LEAST HE DIDN'T HAVE TO EXPERIENCE... THIS PAIN...

...THAT I DIDN'T BRING... SILVER WITH ME... THAT I HAD HIM TELEPORTED TO A SAFE PLACE...

I... I'M GLAD... HHH... HHH...

JUST AS I WAS TELE-PORTED FROM THAT PLACE...

I'VE... GOTTEN STRONGER... THAN YOU THINK....

BUT... I TELE-PORTED YOU TO SAFETY...

NNGH... GREEN... HHH... HHH...

SILVER ...!! SILVER ...!!

YOU'VE ALWAYS BEEN SO WELL PREPARED. I HAD A FEELING... THAT YOU WOULD HAVE RESEARCHED THE PLACE... IN ADVANCE...

IT WAS A... **FLOWER MAIL** WITH NOTES WRITTEN ON IT.

YOU MEAN... YOU USED THIEF ON A POKÉMON ?!

GET
VER...
HAT
?!

IT FEELS
SO GOOD
TO GET
OVER
THAT!

I SHOULD
THANK
YOU FOR
THIS. IN
FACT...
THANKS!
♡

!!

...BECAUSE
THERE WAS
SOMETHING
I HAD TO DO.
SOMETHING
I HAD TO
OVERCOME!

I DISAPPEARED
AND LEFT SILVER
TO WRAP THINGS
UP AFTER THE
BATTLE AGAINST
THE ELITE FOUR...

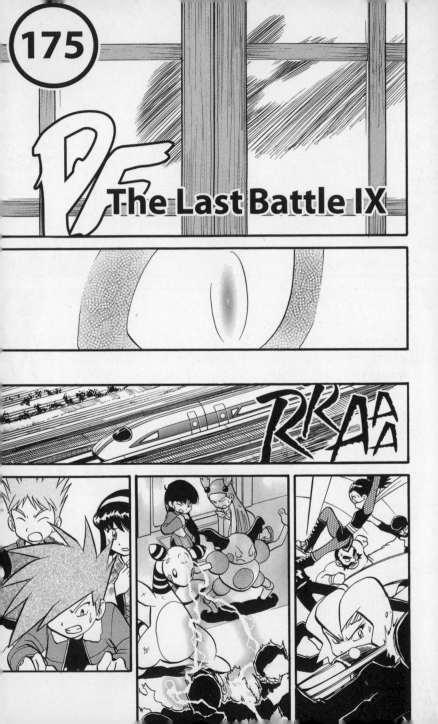

MAS- TER!

OKAY THEN... WE'D BETTER GET BACK THERE RIGHT AWAY!

TERRIBLY, THAT'S HOW!

HOW'S THE LEAGUE TOURN- AMENT GOING?

GO!! OH, AND BLUE... I'M COUNTING ON YOU!!

P**OOM**

NO PROBLEM! I'LL HOLD OFF NEO TEAM ROCKET!!

MY NEW POKÉMON— A GROUND- TYPE. IT CAN TUNNEL US THROUGH THE GROUND WITH ITS DRILL!!

A RHY- DON ?!

GET ON!!

GWN

WHO KNOWS WHAT KIND OF TRAPS THEY'VE LAID FOR US ABOVE GROUND!

B**O** M

116

SO THIS IS OUR DESTINATION ...

GGGGG

KR EK

OOK !!

!!

MUST BE. THE PLACE THE LEGEND DESCRIBED ...

MAYBE THIS IS WHAT BRUNO WAS TALKING ABOUT ...

"HERE LIVES THE PROTEC- TOR OF THE FOREST"

"ILEX FOREST SHRINE.

177 The Last Battle XI

HOOOO !!

AAAAH !!

...THOSE ARE THE LEGENDARY POKÉMON LUGIA AND HO-OH!

RED!

NOT TO MENTION FIGHTING BESIDE GREEN— WHO HAS A PHOBIA OF FLYING POKÉMON...

WHAT ARE ALL OF YOU DOING IN ILEX FOREST?

LONG TIME NO SEE, ARTI-CUNO!

YOU MEAN ...?

AND IF YOU OBSERVE THEIR MOVEMENTS CLOSELY... IT'S OBVIOUS THEY'RE TRYING TO KEEP PEOPLE FROM ENTERING THE FOREST.

AND THE ONE WHO'S TRYING TO STOP THEM IS...

GREEN !!

...MUST BE WHAT THAT GUY WHO ATTACKED THE TOURNAMENT IS LOOKING FOR! HE MUST HAVE STATIONED THOSE TWO POKÉMON HERE TO PREVENT ANYBODY FROM INTERFERING!!

RIGHT! THIS TIME TRAVEL POKÉMON CELEBI...

147

OH! OOK!!

IT'S PRYCE'S CANE!!

WHAT'S THIS?

THERE'S A SPECIAL POKÉGEAR INSIDE IT!!

IT'S GOT AN ANTENNA! AND A LITTLE SCREEN TOO!!

PAK

WHAT DO YOU MEAN?

SO THAT'S HOW HE DID IT...

!!

BUT... WHAT WAS HE WATCHING ON THIS THING...?

150

RIGHT? PRYCE WAS WITH US TOO!

ALL THE GYM LEADERS WERE RIGHT HERE WHEN THE IMAGE OF THE TIN TOWER CAME UP ON THE SCREEN!

THERE MUST HAVE BEEN A CAMERA IN THE DOLL'S EYE, AND THE IMAGE WAS SENT TO THE POKÉGEAR PRYCE WAS USING TO WATCH WHAT WAS GOING ON.

HE SHOWED US THE IMAGE OF HIS ICE DOLL, HIS DOUBLE, FIGHTING OUTSIDE THE TIN TOWER!

AND THAT WAS H PLAN A ALONG

THAT'S HOW HE WAS ABLE TO APPEAR TO BE HAVING A POKÉMON BATTLE SOMEWHERE ELSE WHILE HE WAS HERE ON INDIGO PLATEAU!

YES!

DOUB ... ICE DOLL

I THOUGHT IT WAS JUST A HABIT, BUT NOW I KNOW WHY HE DID IT.

PRYCE KEPT HITTING HIS CANE ON THE GROUND LIKE THIS ...

LET ME BORROW THIS FOR A SEC...

BUT HOW D HE GIV ORDER TO HI POKÉ MON

TOK KON

151

HEY! ARE YOU OKAY?
OH! YOU SAVED PIKA AND CHUCHU'S EGG!
AM I OKAY...? HUF...HUF... YOU LOOK PRETTY BEAT UP YOURSELF.
YEAH, VE GOT TTACKED TOO...
BY NEO TEAM ROCKET TROOPS... WHO ARE UNDER HIS CONTROL!
WHAT ...?! URGH ...
OWWWW!
OH, GOLD!! IF YOU'RE GOING TO KEEP FIGHTING, YOU HAD BETTER READ THIS!
IT'S FROM PRO-FESSOR OAK!
VHAT?! HANKS!! I BET THIS'LL ELL ME OW TO EFEAT OUR ENEMY !!
WELL... I DON'T THINK SO...
TO GOLD
HE GAVE THIS TO ME A WHILE AGO. SAID TO PASS IT ON TO YOU WHEN NEXT I SAW YOU.
WHAT ...?
The Fighter (Pokémon Battle)
The Healer (Pokémon Healing)
The Catcher (Pokémon Capturing)
The Evolver (Pokémon Evolution
The Exchanger (Pokémon Trading)
WHAT IS THIS?

AS A STUDENT OF THE RELATIONSHIPS BETWEEN POKÉMON AND THEIR TRAINERS, I'VE KEPT MY EYES ON TRAINERS' AREAS OF EXPERTISE.

EACH ONE OF THOSE SKILLS IS VERY IMPORTANT.

EVERYONE WHO'S GONE ON A QUEST WITH A POKÉDEX HAS A PARTICULAR SKILL THEY EXCEL IN.

CRYS. SHE TRULY CATCHES THEM ALL. "THE CATCHER."

YELLOW. CLEARLY "THE HEALER."

BLUE. A MASTER AT TRAINING POKÉMON. "THE TRAINER."

RED. A BATTLE SPECIALIST WHO HAS WON THE POKÉMON LEAGUE TOURNAMENT. "THE FIGHTER."

!!

THEY'RE ALL BETTER THAN ME IN SOME WAY... BUT WHY ARE YOU TELLING ME THIS?

I'VE HEARD ALL THOSE NAMES BEFORE FROM CRYS.

JUDGING FROM WHAT GREEN TOLD ME ABOUT HER PAST, I ASSUME SILVER WAS THE ONE WHO STOLE MY NEW POKÉDEX.

THEN THERE'S GREEN. AND SILVER, WHO THINKS OF GREEN AS AN ELDER SISTER.

158

160

164

SHHH

BDMP BDMP BDMP

CHOOSE A NEW PARTNER... FROM THE TRAINERS HERE...

I'M SORRY, BUT I DON'T HAVE ENOUGH STRENGTH LEFT...TO GO WITH YOU...

M-ME?

I HAD A HUNCH... THE MOMENT I SAW YOU WITH JUST ONE EARRING!

SUICUNE MUST HAVE DECIDED LONG BEFORE...

I KNEW IT...

HAHAHA! SUICUNE HAD IT ALL THIS TIME...

!! TH-THIS IS...?!

PUP

FWAH

LOOKS LIKE YOU'RE IN PRETTY BAD SHAPE.

...OU ...OO.

AH!!

MY GOOD FRIEND !!

HEEEY! EUSINE !!

SNFF

...GHT ...

I did save it, after all!

SO THE NEXT PARTNER IT'LL CHOOSE WILL DEFINITELY BE ME.

I'M CONFIDENT SUICUNE HAS A VIVID MEMORY OF WHAT I DID TODAY.

YEAH! ARE YOU SURE ABOUT LETTING SUICUNE GO...?

LONG TIME NO SEE!

BUT I'M A GYM LEADER.

NO ...

AND YOU COULDN'T KEEP YOUR COOL WHEN YOU SAW HO-OH, COULD YOU?

MY JOB IS TO PROTECT OTHERS... NOT TO CHASE AFTER MY DREAMS!

... SUDDENLY APPEARED ON THE SCREEN AT THE TOURNA- MENT...

WHEN THE RAINBOW POKÉMON I'D BEEN SEARCH- ING FOR MY WHOLE LIFE...

I heard you say there was an attack on the tournament, and then the radio stopped working. What happened? I'm scared.

Pancha, Violet City

THE FAX MACHINE IS STILL WORKING...

BEEE

NEW-TON, SAF-FRON CITY."

"I WISH I COULD GET TO INDIGO PLATEAU TO HELP THE GYM LEADERS!

"I'M STILL LISTENING TO THE RADIO. AMY, BLACK-THORN CITY"

"IS IT TRUE THAT A BAD GUY JUST TURNED THE TOURNAMENT UPSIDE DOWN?"

THESE FAXES ARE FROM TRAINERS IN THE LISTENING AUDIENCE...

THE BROADCAST CONTINUED AFTER THE ATTACK...

178

179

POKÉMON CENTER

AZALEA
TOWN

THANKS, BLUE.

ARE YOU OKAY, GREEN...?!

...WE'D BE IN RANGE TO USE ZAPDOS'S ELECTRIC ATTACKS AND ARTICUNO'S ICE ATTACKS!!

IF WE COULD GET JUST A LITTLE CLOSER TO LUGIA AND HO-OH...

WE'RE GOING TO HAVE TO THINK OF A NEW PLAN!

BUT WE CAN'T GET ANY CLOSER THAN WE ARE NOW!!

JNNNN

TP

VOoo

TCH!!

YEAH! NOTHING CAN STOP POKÉMON WHEN THEY WORK TOGETHER!!

THEY'VE BEEN FREED FROM THE MASKED MAN'S CONTROL!

THEY'RE HEADING BACK INTO THE SKY.

LISTEN, GREEN!

HE WANTED TO KEEP US AWAY FROM THAT SHRINE. WELL, TOO LATE NOW!

HUH?

COULD YOU PUT ARTICUNO, ZAPDOS AND MOLTRES INTO YOUR POKÉ BALLS?

VSH

PAP

PAP

PAP

SURE.

"GOTTA CATCH 'EM ALL!!"
ADVENTURE ROUTE MAP 14

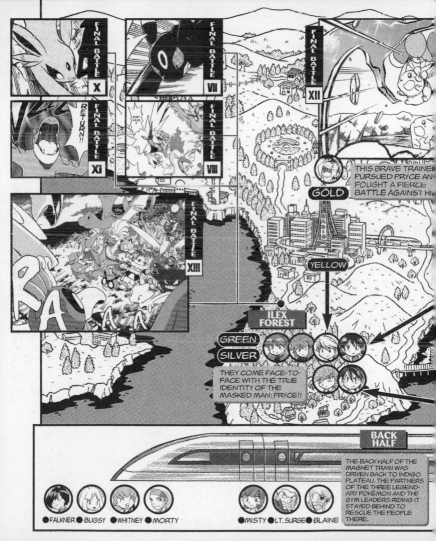

FINAL BATTLE X

FINAL BATTLE XI — RETURN!!

FINAL BATTLE VII

FINAL BATTLE VIII

FINAL BATTLE XIII

FINAL BATTLE XII

GOLD — THIS BRAVE TRAINER PURSUED PRYCE AND FOUGHT A FIERCE BATTLE AGAINST HIM

YELLOW

ILEX FOREST

GREEN

SILVER

THEY COME FACE-TO-FACE WITH THE TRUE IDENTITY OF THE MASKED MAN: PRYCE!!

BACK HALF

THE BACK HALF OF THE MAGNET TRAIN WAS DRIVEN BACK TO INDIGO PLATEAU. THE PARTNERS OF THE THREE LEGEND-ARY POKÉMON AND THE GYM LEADERS RIDING IT STAYED BEHIND TO RESCUE THE PEOPLE THERE.

● FALKNER ● BUGSY ● WHITNEY ● MORTY ● MISTY ● LT. SURGE ● BLAINE

This is the Masked Man!!

~An Analysis in Five Parts~

THE TRUE IDENTITY OF THE MASKED MAN HAS FINALLY BEEN REVEALED. LET'S TAKE A CLOSER LOOK AT PRYCE, THE ICE EXPERT!

01 Goal

PRYCE'S GOAL IS TO CAPTURE THE TIME TRAVEL POKÉMON CELEBI IN ORDER TO CONTROL TIME. KIDNAPPING CHILDREN AND CONTROLLING THE SOLDIERS OF NEO TEAM ROCKET WERE NOTHING BUT MEANS TO THAT END!

...AND WITH GOOD REASON...

▲ SUICUNE INSTINCTIVELY SENSED WHAT KIND OF A MAN PRYCE WAS AND AVOIDED HIM.

02 Double

PRYCE IS AN OLD MAN WHO RARELY GOES OUTSIDE, SO HE CARVED AN ICE DOLL AS A DOUBLE TO CARRY OUT HIS PLANS. THE DOLL LED HIS ICE-TYPE POKÉMON IN BATTLES AND CAPTURES.

◄ PRYCE WAS EVEN ▼ ▲ ABLE TO CAPTURE A LEGENDARY POKÉMON WITHOUT BEING PRESENT IN PERSON! (ADV. 149 AND OTHERS)

164 Slick Slowking

THE RAINBOW-COLORED WINGS... IT'S THE LEGENDARY POKÉMON OF BORUTAW...

HO-OH!

...AND LUGIA GOT CAUGHT BY SOMEONE ELSE!

MAYBE... IT CAN'T TRACK A POKÉMON WHO'S BEEN CAPTURED.

03 Equipment

THIS MECHANICAL CANE WAS PRYCE'S TOOL TO CONTROL HIS ICE DOLL DOUBLE. A SPECIAL POKÉGEAR HAS BEEN IMPLANTED INSIDE IT, ENABLING PRYCE TO SEE WHATEVER HIS DOUBLE SEES. PRYCE INGENIOUSLY SENT ORDERS TO HIS POKÉMON BY TAPPING THE TIP OF THE CANE ON THE FLOOR. (SEE ADV. 178)

◄ BY COMBINING SHORT AND LONG TONES, HE COMMUNICATES THROUGH A SORT OF MORSE CODE. HE NEVER SPEAKS HIS ORDERS.

KLANK

TONG TONG

TK

POKÉGEAR

A WHEELCHAIR WITH SPECIAL NON-SLIP TIRES. THERE'S ANOTHER SECRET GIMMICK IN THOSE TIRES YET TO BE REVEALED!

PRYCE'S CELEBI-CAPTURING TEAM INCLUDES TYPES THAT ARE NOT HIS SPECIALTY. (SEE ADV. 103)

STAY AWAY... FROM THIS FOREST.

04 Poké-mon

VERY LITTLE IS KNOWN ABOUT CELEBI, THE POKÉMON PRYCE IS AFTER, BUT IT SEEMS TO BE A GRASS-TYPE OR PSYCHIC-TYPE POKÉMON; THEREFORE, PRYCE BRINGS FIRE-, ICE-, POISON-TYPE AND FLYING-TYPE POKÉMON WITH HIM BECAUSE THEY ARE STRONG AGAINST GRASS-TYPE POKÉMON, AND BUG-, GHOST- AND DARK-TYPE POKÉMON BECAUSE THEY ARE STRONG AGAINST PSYCHIC-TYPE POKÉMON.

05 Body

PRYCE DRAWS ON THE WATER IN THE ATMOS-PHERE TO CREATE HIS BODY DOUBLE. WHENEVER HE NEEDS TO GO OUT HIMSELF, HE COVERS HIS WHEELCHAIR WITH ICE AND WEARS A CAPE OVER IT TO HIDE HIS BODY...CREATING AN EVERLASTING ICE WALL THAT CAN REGENERATE ITSELF EVEN IF PARTS OF HIS BODY ARE DESTROYED! (SEE ADV. 172)

PRYCE'S SIZE VARIED EVERY TIME HE APPEARED, WHICH MADE IT HARDER FOR PEOPLE TO FIGURE OUT HIS IDENTITY.

FSHOOO

COMPLETE! THE POKÉ BALL THAT CAPTURES TIME!!

A SPECIAL POKÉ BALL PRYCE CREATED TO CAPTURE CELEBI, WITH A CAPTURE NET WOVEN OUT OF THE RAINBOW WING AND SILVER WING. HE MIGHT BE ABLE TO TAKE CONTROL OF TIME YET!

▲ THE ILEX FOREST SHRINE, WHICH CELEBI USES AS AN ENTRANCE TO OUR WORLD.

▶ WITH THE AID OF THESE TWO FEATHERS, HE WAS ABLE TO OPEN THE "CRACK IN TIME". (SEE ADV. 178)

HYOOO

THE SEVEN TRAINERS WHO RECEIVED POKÉDEXES FROM PROFESSOR OAK. EACH OF THEM HAS A UNIQUE AREA OF EXPERTISE. AND THOSE EXPERTISES ARE...?!

01 The Fighter

RED. A FIGHTING GENIUS WITH A NATURAL INSTINCT FOR COMBAT AND STRATEGY WHO HAS WON THE POKÉMON LEAGUE TOURNAMENT. HIS SPECIAL ABILITY IS POKÉMON BATTLE!!

PSYCH UP!!

▶ A UNIQUE TACTIC IN WHICH HE USES HIS OPPONENTS' ATTACKS AGAINST THEM.

02 The Trainer

YOU'LL NEVER FIND ANYBODY AS GOOD AS BLUE WHEN IT COMES TO TRAINING POKÉMON. HIS POKÉMON TRAINING ABILITY WAS ATTAINED THROUGH HARD PRACTICE!

YOUR TRAINING OF THIS POKÉMON IS AS SUCCESSFUL AS ANYONE COULD ASK FOR...

ESPECIALLY CONSIDERING THAT YOU BASICALLY STARTED FROM SCRATCH.

▲ HE PARTICIPATED IN THE TOURNAMENT WITH A TEAM HE HAD NEWLY TRAINED. HIS MASTER THINKS HIGHLY OF HIM TOO. (SEE ADV. 162)

03 The Healer

YELLOW. THE WIELDER OF A GENTLE POWER WHICH CAN HEAL AND CHEER UP WOUNDED POKÉMON. THIS POKÉMON HEALING ABILITY WAS BESTOWED UPON HER BY THE VIRIDIAN FOREST.

GLEEM

▲ SHE IS ABLE TO HEAL WOUNDS WITHOUT THE ASSISTANCE OF THE POKÉMON CENTER MACHINES.

04 The Catcher

CRYS. HER SKILLS AS A CAPTURE SPECIALIST ARE LEGENDARY. SHE MASTERED HER POKÉMON CAPTURING SKILL BY TRAINING FROM HER EARLY CHILDHOOD ON!

PHANPHY... AND MAGBY

WIIIN

▲ VARIOUS POKÉ BALLS SENT BY HER TO PROVIDE RESEARCH DATA. (ADV. 121)

05 The Ex-changer

06 The Evolver

THE ARTS SILVER AND GREEN STUDIED UNDER THE MASKED MAN ARE TRADING AND EVOLUTION. THESE TWO ABILITIES ARE OFTEN TALKED ABOUT AS A PAIR. IN SOME WAYS, THE TWO OF THEM TOGETHER MAKE UP ONE ABILITY.

▼THIS SITUATION WAS SIMILAR TO WHAT HAPPENED IN SILPH CO. THREE YEARS AGO. SILVER RECALLS THE INFORMATION ABOUT EVOLVING WHICH GREEN TAUGHT HIM.

WHEN POKÉMON AT SIMILAR EVOLUTIONARY LEVELS HANG OUT TOGETHER, THEY GET COMPETITIVE... SO COMPETITIVE IT ACCELERATES THEIR GROWTH.

WHIRLPOOL!!

▲ BY EXCHANGING THEIR POKEMON, THEY MADE A NARROW ESCAPE. SILVER'S QUICK THINKING CAME INTO PLAY. (SEE ADV. 109)

▼ GREEN IS AN EXPERT ON USING EVOLUTION STONES TO EVOLVE POKÉMON. (SEE ADV. 32)

I'VE HEARD OF THAT... BUT I'VE NEVER ACTUALLY...

BUT I'LL DO A TRADE... BECAUSE I'M SUCH A SWEETHEART! I'LL GIVE YOU THIS BADGE FOR YOUR MOON STONE!

07 The Hatcher

THE ABILITY TO HATCH A POKÉMON EGG. HATCHING WAS GOLD'S HIDDEN ABILITY, ONE HE DIDN'T EVEN REALIZE HE HAD. GOLD WILL INFLUENCE THE BABY POKÉMON WELL, DRAWING OUT THE BEST OF THEIR ABILITIES.

▲HATCHED THANKS TO THE EFFORT TO BEST SILVER. (SEE ADV. 107)

GOLD ▶ HAS DISAPPEARED ALONG WITH THE NEWLY HATCHED POKÉMON. WHERE COULD HE BE...?!

HATCHED ▶ FROM THE EGG THAT WAS PROTECTED FROM PRYCE. (SEE ADV. 178)

PWOK

180

The Last Battle XIV

THE

LAST

BATTLES

PONK

THAT'S NOT ALL...

ICE SHIELDS !!

WHA ?!

SIX OF THEM!

THE SHIELDS ARE GATHERING MOISTURE FROM THE AIR AND... MAKING ICE DOLLS!

GO, MY DOLLS !!

SHK

MRK

WMM

SHK

HEH... THE BOY DID WELL.

AH, GOLD.

GOLD WHER ARE YOU?

SILVER!

BRRRB

?!

SSSSS

DOES THIS MEAN THAT GOLD IS...

HIS **FLASH** ATTACK WAS SO POWERFUL THAT I'M STILL NEARLY BLIND.

HE RIPPED MY MASK OFF AND TRIED TO DRAG ME DOWN AS I ENTERED THE CRACK IN TIM

POKÉ DEX?

TAKE A LOOK AT THE POKÉ DEX!!

IS THAT YOU, SILVER? YOU REALLY ARE A GOOD STUDENT, AREN'T YOU? BECAUSE... YOU'RE **RIGHT!**

HE MIGHT!!

YOU MEAN... HE MIGHT BE HERE AFTER ALL?

EVEN THE POKÉDEX ISN'T SURE IF GOLD IS HERE OR NOT!

THE RESONANC LIGHT IS BLINKING, BUT...THE RESONANC ALERT ISN' RINGING!

213

218

222

NNH...

HFF... WEEZ...

OKAY, NOW... LET'S GET INTO THAT SHRINE!!

I THOUGHT YOU STOLE MY BACKPACK... THAT'S WHERE ALL THIS STARTED.

HEY... THAT'S US...AT NEW BARK TOWN.

WHAT BACK-PACK?

GIVE ME MY BACK-PACK!!

...I DON'T THINK I'M GONNA... HFF... MAKE IT OUT OF HERE...

GLAD I... NNH... GOT A CHANCE TO SAY THAT... 'CAUSE...

I'M SORRY, OKAY?

HEH... GUESS I FORGOT TO MENTION IT, BUT... I KINDA JUMPED TO CONCLUSIONS...

♫ LET OLD PASSIONS FLY.

LOVE THE ONES THAT YOU HAVE LOST. ♫

THE MAN WHO WRECKED THE TOURNAMENT... THE MASTERMIND BEHIND EVERYTHING... **YOU'VE KNOWN HIM FOR YEARS?!**

ARE YOU SERIOUS, OLD LADY?!

KURT ON THE LEFT...

THAT'S ME IN THE MIDDLE...

SAM-UEL...

AGA-THA...

AND AFTER GOLD CALLED HIS NAME...I KNEW I WAS RIGHT.

I HAD A HUNCH WHEN I SAW A SHADOW DISAPPEAR INTO THE SKY ON THE WAY HERE.

WE WERE YOUNG THEN... OUR FUTURES SEEMED SO BRIGHT...

LOOK AT THIS PHOTO.

PRYCE.

...ME!! WHY'S THAT SO HARD TO BELIEVE?!

THE SIX OF US WERE SUCH GOOD FRIENDS.

DON'T TELL ME THAT CUTE CHICK NEXT TO YOU IS...

TAKE IT OUT OF THE FRAME AND LOOK AGAIN.

SIX? BUT THERE ARE ONLY FIVE OF YOU IN THIS—

BUT ONE DAY... SOMETHING HAPPENED THAT ENDED ALL THAT.

AND WE DID.

NONE OF US KNEW WHAT WE WANTED TO DO IN THE FUTURE. WE JUST WANTED TO HAVE FUN.

RE-SEARCHER, POKÉ BALL CRAFTS-MAN, BREEDER, GYM LEADER.

KURT AND I WROTE THE LYRICS. AGATHA AND SAMUEL MADE THE MUSIC.

WE DECIDED TO COMPOSE A SONG, A BALLAD, JUST FOR PRYCE.

HE NEVER FORGAVE HIMSELF. HE WITHDREW FROM ALL OF US. SO WE TRIED TO COME UP WITH A WAY TO CHEER HIM UP...

PRYCE LOST TWO OF HIS BELOVED LAPRAS AT THE ICE FIELD.

AND WHAT DID YOU DO, OLD LADY?

241

L... ...OOK !!

HOOOO...!

WHAT HAPPENED INSIDE THE SHRINE— INSIDE THE CRACK IN TIME?

AFTER WE ATTACKED, I FELT A HUGE EXPLOSION OF ENERGY!

CRYS! RAIKOU! SUICUNE! ENTEI!

AND SILVER !!

BUT HE GAVE HIS OWN LIFE TO DO IT.

HE STOPPED PRYCE... AND RELEASED CELEBI.

!!!

BLUE ...?

GET A HOLD OF YOUR-SELF!

GRP

NH...

WOBBLE

W... WAIT...! STOP IT!!

I'VE HAD MY EYE ON YOU SINCE I SAW YOU AT THE TOURNA-MENT.

JERK

ARE YOU DONE TALKING? THEN YOU'RE COMING WITH ME!!

BUT HE HAD NO CHOICE !!

YES, IT WAS WRONG OF HIM TO DO THOSE THINGS ...!

I'M BRINGING YOU IN FOR THE THEFT OF A POKÉDEX FROM PROF. OAK AND THE KIDNAPPING OF A TOTODILE FROM PROF. ELM'S LAB!

246

248

IT WAS AWFULLY CLEVER OF ME TO GET AWAY FROM MOLTRES THE MOMENT WE SAW ALL THOSE POKÉMON!

I GUESS EVEN WEAKLINGS CAN BE POWERFUL IN GROUPS.

WELL, THAT WAS QUITE A SUR- PRISE.

TP

FWH FWH

MAYBE YOU SHOULD JOIN US ...

HUH ?

BUT HOW ARE WE GOING TO HAVE ANY FUN ANYMORE WITHOUT PRYCE?

A COUPLE OF GUYS WHO USED TO BE JUST LIKE YOU.

AND YOU ARE ...?

I'M KOGA. I'M LEFT OVER FROM THE OLD TEAM ROCKET.

AND I'M BRUNO. A LEFTOVER FROM THE KANTO ELITE FOUR.

251

253

DUE TO THE WRECKAGE AT INDIGO PLATEAU, THE TOURNAMENT IS CANCELED, LEAVING ITS MARK ON HISTORY AS THE "TOURNAMENT WITH NO CHAMPION."

AS FOR THE KANTO VS. JOHTO GYM LEADERS' MATCH...CLAIR REPORTS THAT SHE LOST THE UNOFFICIAL 7TH MATCH ON THE MAGNET TRAIN. SO, WITH 4 WINS, 3 LOSSES AND 1 DRAW, KANTO IS DECLARED THE WINNER.

ALL THIS, NATURALLY, CAUSES THE NUMBER OF TRAINERS WHO ATTEMPT TO EARN BADGES FROM GYM LEADERS SO THEY CAN ENTER THE TOURNAMENT TO SKYROCKET...AND SO THE LEADERS FIND THEMSELVES BUSIER THAN EVER.

HAVING LEARNED OF THE MASK OF ICE'S SCHEME TO MASTER TIME TRAVEL, BILL SETS OUT TO HARNESS THE SAME POWER FOR THE GOOD OF HUMANITY AND POKÉMON... SPECIFICALLY TO INCORPORATE IT INTO HIS TRANSPORTER SYSTEM. HIS NEW RESEARCH IS GARNERING MUCH SUPPORT.

RAIKOU, ENTEI AND SUICUNE WENT TO SEEK THEIR MASTER HO-OH— AND VANISHED AGAIN. HO-OH AND LUGIA ARE ONCE AGAIN LEGENDARY.

...AND UNLESS THEY'RE FOUND, THE ILEX FOREST SHRINE WILL NEVER BE OPENED AGAIN.

THE RAINBOW WING AND SILVER WING HAVE BEEN LOST, PERHAPS FOREVER...

SO THE STORY OF THE MASK OF ICE WHO SHOOK THE JOHTO AND KANTO REGIONS TO THEIR BEDROCK COMES TO A CLOSE.

AND NOW...

. . .

Mmg.... Nnh...?
What time is it...?
Can you take a look at the
clock for me...?

Where's the hour hand?
10 O'clock.

What...? 10 O'clock?!

And the minute hand?
At 35 minutes.

35?!
You're sure it's 35?!

10:35!
I can't believe this!

VOOM

I OVER-SLEPT!!

OH. DID YOU TELL ME TO WAKE YOU UP, PROFESSOR?

CRYS, WHY DIDN'T YOU WAKE ME UP?!

I'VE GOT TO GET TO GOLDENROD FOR MY LIVE RADIO BROADCAST!

HERE! LOOK!

FINALLY? WONDERFUL! UM... DID WHAT?

OH, PROFESSOR! I FINALLY DID IT!

I MISS DAISY...

SIGH... DAISY ALWAYS WOKE ME UP WHETHER I ASKED HER TO OR NOT.

I COULDN'T CAPTURE THE LEGENDARY POKÉMON, OF COURSE, BUT I MANAGED TO GATHER MOST OF THEIR DATA DURING THE BATTLE. AND THE REST WAS PRETTY EASY.

SO HERE YOU GO...

I COMPLETED THE POKÉDEX!!

...COLLECTION COMPLETED!!

YOU WHAT?!

Hello! Im Professor Oak, and I'll be your guide to the secrets of Pokémon!

This world is inhabited far and wide by creatures called Pokémon! For some people Pokémon are pets. Others...

...use them for battling! As for myself...I study Pokémon as a profession.

But there is still so much we don't know about them... so many secrets yet to be discovered!

And so I have devoted my life to discovering new Pokémon and learning more about the ones we know!

Wants a Pokédex and to become a Trainer and spend lots of time with Pokémon!
Prof!
A kid wants to see you!
ON AIR
All right... Tell me a little about yourself.
What's your name...?

Pokémon Adventures

RED GREEN BLUE · YELLOW · GOLD SILVER & CRYSTAL

Fin

TRAINER DATA

GREEN

BLASTOISE	BLASTOISE ♂	Lv70
JIGGLY	JIGGLYPUFF ♀	Lv57
DITTO	DITTO	Lv40
CLEFABLE	CLEFABLE ♂	Lv60
NIDO	NIDORINA ♀	Lv59
SNUBBULL	SNUBBULL ♂	Lv22

OTHER MEMBERS

ABRA ♀	Lv 15	

BLUE

CHARIZARD	CHARIZARD ♂	Lv81
SCIZOR	SCIZOR ♂	Lv80
PORYGON2	PORYGON2	Lv61
GOLDUCK	GOLDUCK ♂	Lv79
RHYDON	RHYDON ♂	Lv71
PIDGEOT	PIDGEOT ♂	Lv76

OTHER MEMBERS

NINETALES ♂	Lv 68	
MACHAMP ♂	Lv 70	
EXEGGUTOR ♂	Lv 67	
ALAKAZAM ♂	Lv 64	
ARCANINE ♂	Lv 71	

RED

SAUR	VENUSAUR ♂	Lv72
POLI	POLIWRATH ♂	Lv70
PIKA	PIKACHU ♂	Lv85
GYARA	GYARADOS ♂	Lv74
LAX	SNORLAX ♂	Lv86
AERO	AERODACTYL ♂	Lv76

OTHER MEMBERS

ESPEON ♂	Lv 65	
DIGLETT ♂	Lv 23	
SANDSHREW ♂	Lv 21	
NIDORINO ♂	Lv 42	

TRAINER DATA

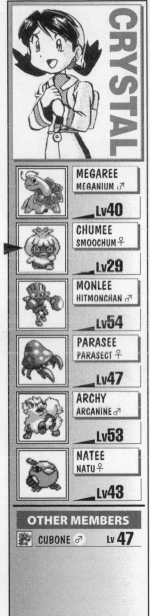

CRYSTAL

	MEGAREE MEGANIUM ♂	Lv40
	CHUMEE SMOOCHUM ♀	Lv29
	MONLEE HITMONCHAN ♂	Lv54
	PARASEE PARASECT ♀	Lv47
	ARCHY ARCANINE ♂	Lv53
	NATEE NATU ♀	Lv43

OTHER MEMBERS
CUBONE ♂   Lv 47

SILVER

	FERALIGATR FERALIGATR ♂	Lv45
	SNEASEL SNEASEL ♂	Lv46
	KINGDRA KINGDRA ♀	Lv44
	GYARADOS GYARADOS ♂	Lv40
	URSARING URSARING ♂	Lv44
	MURKROW MURKROW ♂	Lv43

OTHER MEMBERS

YELLOW

	CHUCHU PIKACHU ♀	Lv31
	RATTY RATICATE ♂	Lv25
	DODY DODRIO ♂	Lv33
	OMNY OMANYTE ♂	Lv42
	GRAVVY GOLEM ♂	Lv39
	KITTY BUTTERFREE ♂	Lv20

OTHER MEMBERS

TRAINER DATA

SUDOBO	SUDOWOODO ♂	Lv44
TIBO	MANTINE ♂	Lv28

BOX MEMBER

TOGEBO	TOGEPI ♂	Lv25

EXBO	TYPHLOSION ♂	Lv43
AIBO	AIPOM ♂	Lv42
POLIBO	POLITOED ♂	Lv43
SUNBO	SUNFLORA ♀	Lv39

GOLD

Message from
Hidenori Kusaka

Thanks to all your support, this manga
has finally reached volume 14. If
we just count the Gold, Silver and
Crystal episodes, we have seven
volumes. Oh! Come to think of it...
the Red, Blue and Green episodes
plus the Yellow episodes total seven
volumes also! Hmm! So...Part 3 of *Pokémon
Adventures* is actually longer than Parts 1 and 2
combined! Well, anyway, this volume is the finale of this
story arc! I hope you enjoy this special action-packed
volume of *Pokémon Adventures*!!

Message from
Satoshi Yamamoto

Pokémon Adventures...an ensemble
action-adventure in which the
seven main Pokémon Trainers,
Gym Leaders, and supporting cast
members each have a story... Finally
all their stories will come together
and every mystery will be resolved!
Pay attention to the smallest details in the
corners of the panels... Share the characters' thoughts and
feelings... I'll make you cry along with them!!

More Adventures!!

Pokémon Trainers Pearl and Diamond are starstruck! Their lifelong dream is to floor an audience with their Pokémon comedy act. So how do they wind up as bodyguards to a pampered little rich girl on a quest to reach the peak of Mt. Coronet...?!

Come along and join in the thrills and laughs as *Pokémon Adventures* continues with stories inspired by the video games *Pokémon Diamond, Pearl,* and *Platinum Version*!

VOLS. 1 AND 2 ON SALE NOW!

VOL. 3 AVAILABLE NOW!

What's Better Than Catching Pokémon?

Becoming one!

POKÉMON
Mystery Dungeon
GINJI'S RESCUE TEAM

Ginji is a normal boy until the day he turns into a Torchic and joins Mudkip's Rescue Team. Now he must help any and all Pokémon in need…but will Ginji be able to rescue his human self?

me part of the adventure—and
tery—with *Pokémon Mystery
geon: Ginji's Rescue Team.*
yours today!

w.pokemon.com

THIS IS THE END OF THIS GRAPHIC NOVEL!

To properly enjoy this VIZ Media graphic novel, please turn it around and begin reading from right to left.

This book has been printed in the original Japanese format in order to preserve the orientation of the original artwork. Have fun with it!

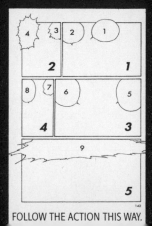

FOLLOW THE ACTION THIS WAY.